ORANGUTANS

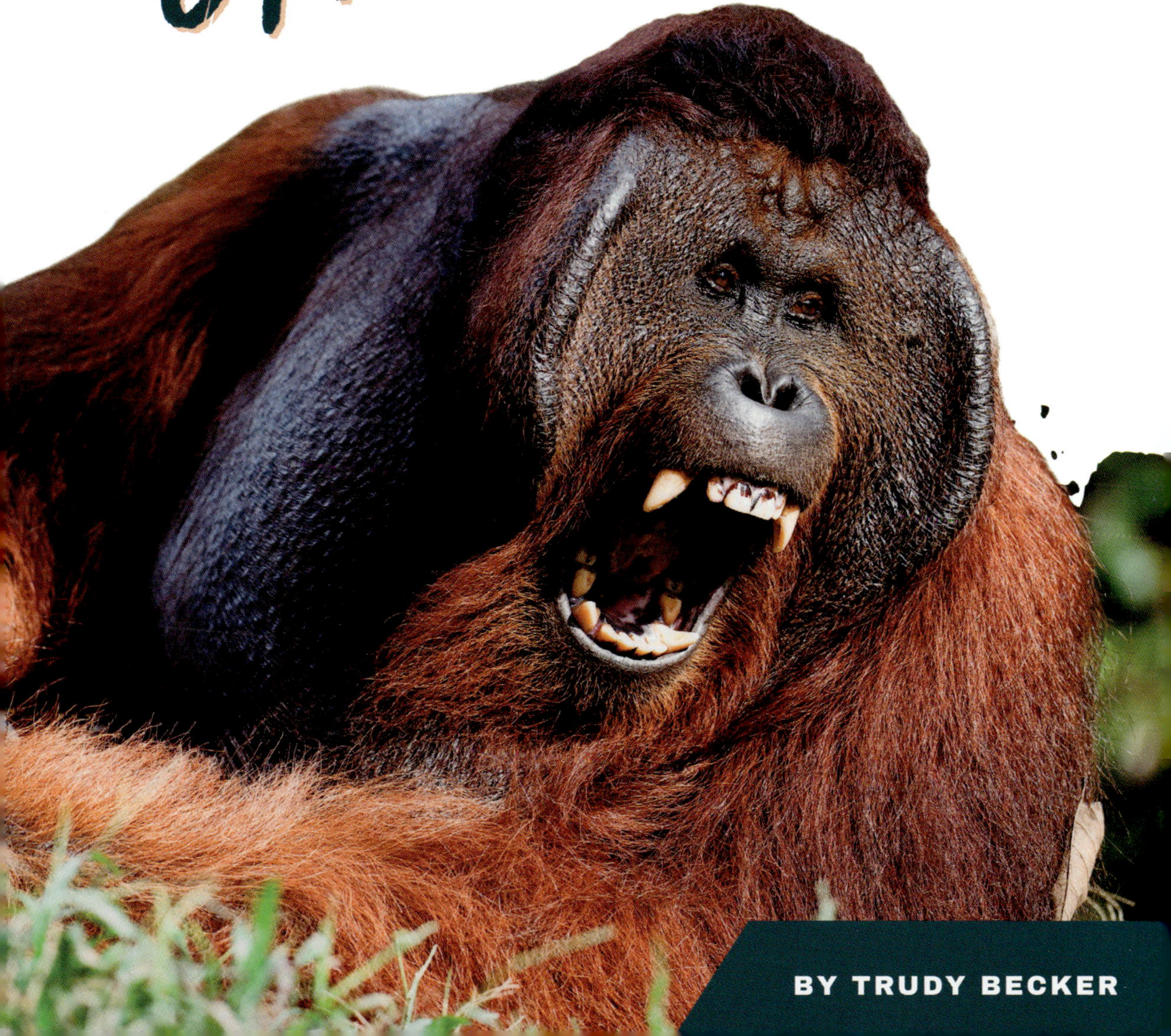

BY TRUDY BECKER

WWW.APEXEDITIONS.COM

Apex is distributed by North Star Editions:
sales@northstareditions.com | 888-417-0195

Produced for Apex by Red Line Editorial.

Photographs ©: Shutterstock Images, cover, 1, 6, 8–9, 10–11, 12–13, 14, 15, 18, 19, 22–23, 24, 26, 29; iStockphoto, 4–5, 16–17, 20–21; Tim Laman/Nature Picture Library/Alamy, 27

Library of Congress Control Number: 2025939161

ISBN
979-8-89250-798-1 (hardcover)
979-8-89250-827-8 (paperback)
979-8-89250-883-4 (ebook pdf)
979-8-89250-856-8 (hosted ebook)

Printed in the United States of America
Mankato, MN
012026

NOTE TO PARENTS AND EDUCATORS

Apex books are designed to build literacy skills in striving readers. Exciting, high-interest content attracts and holds readers' attention. The text is carefully leveled to allow students to achieve success quickly. Additional features, such as bolded glossary words for difficult terms, help build comprehension.

TABLE OF CONTENTS

CHAPTER 1

SCARY SQUEAK

An orangutan sits in a tree in Sumatra. It chews on a fig. Through the branches, it spots a tree python. The large snake slithers closer.

Orangutans can spend up to six hours a day looking for food.

The orangutan grabs a twig and pulls the leaves off. It holds the leaves up to its mouth. It purses its lips. Then it sharply breathes in. A loud squeak rings through the air.

SOUNDING BIGGER

Large orangutans make low-pitched squeaks. **Predators** rarely attack them. So, smaller orangutans try to lower their voices. They use leaves or their hands to make deeper squeaks.

◀ **Predators such as pythons, leopards, and tigers may attack small orangutans.**

The sharp sound scares the python. The snake quickly slithers away. The orangutan is safe. It goes back to eating.

Orangutans may show their sharp teeth to scare off predators.

CHAPTER 2

ALL ABOUT ORANGUTANS

Orangutans are large **primates**. Males may grow 4.3 feet (1.3 m) tall. They can weigh around 285 pounds (130 kg).

Orangutans belong to a group called great apes. These apes have big bodies and brains.

There are three **species** of orangutans. All have very long arms. That helps them climb and swing through trees. Orangutans also have **coarse** red hair.

Some orangutans can stretch their arms 7 feet (2.1 m) wide.

FAST FACT

The word orangutan means "person of the forest" in Malay.

Rainforests in Borneo can get more than 157 inches (400 cm) of rain a year.

Most orangutans are found on Sumatra or Borneo. These islands are in Southeast Asia. The apes live in **tropical** rainforests there.

FACING DANGER

All three types of orangutans are **endangered**. People cut down trees in their habitats. So, the apes have fewer places to live. Hunters may kill orangutans, too.

People often cut down rainforests to plant oil palm trees. Then they sell the trees' palm oil.

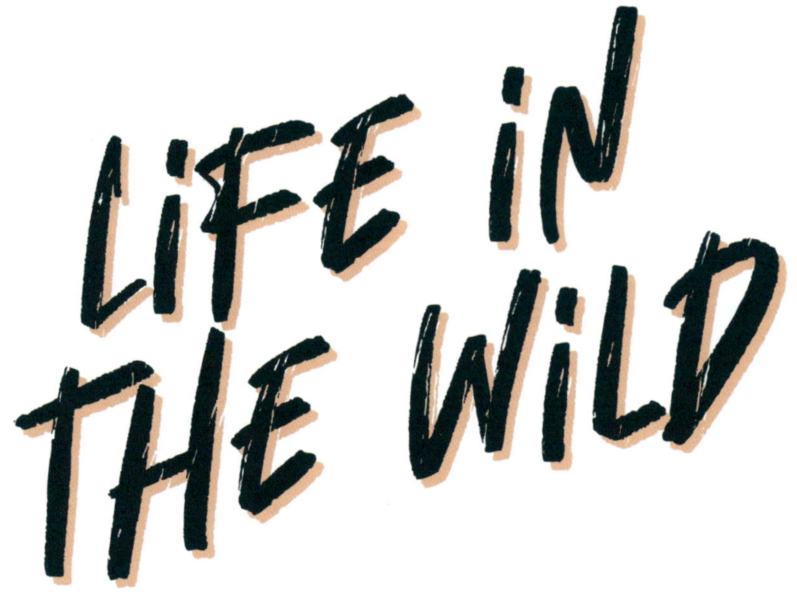

CHAPTER 3

LIFE IN THE WILD

Orangutans eat a lot of fruit. They also eat leaves, bark, and insects. The apes drink water that collects in holes in trees.

Orangutans often eat durian fruit.

Orangutans spend most of their lives up in trees. Each evening, orangutans break off branches, leaves, and twigs. They use these to build a nest to sleep in.

Orangutans are the largest animals that live mainly in trees.

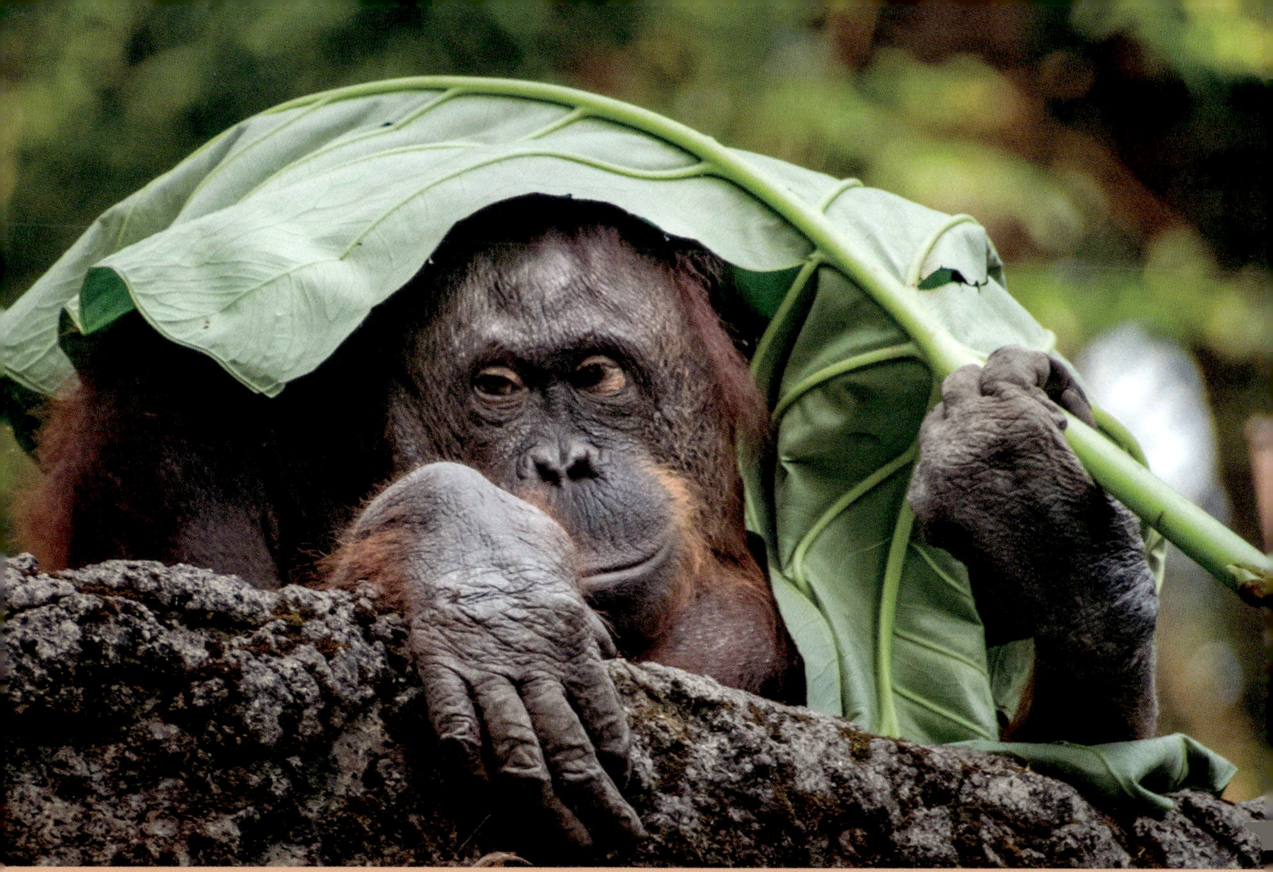

Orangutans may use leaves as umbrellas.

FAST FACT

Orangutans can use tools. For example, some orangutans use sticks to get insects out of holes.

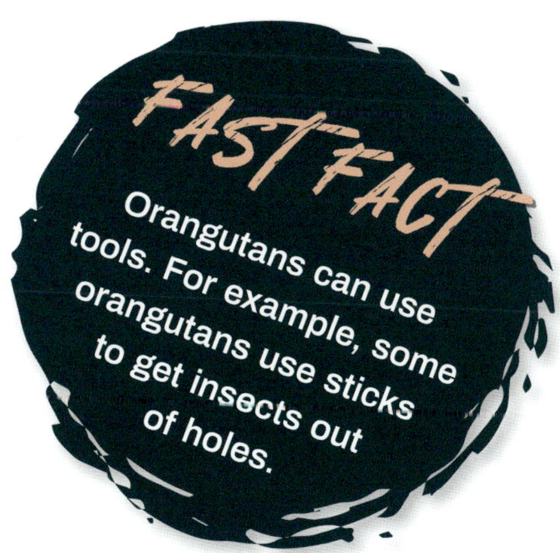

Each adult orangutan has a home range. Sometimes, these areas overlap. Orangutans may join up for a few days to travel or find food. But adults spend most of their time alone.

Some male orangutans use loud calls to mark their land. The sounds can reach 1.2 miles (2 km) away. When other males hear a call, they know to stay out of that area.

Larger groups of orangutans may join up in areas with lots of food.

CHAPTER 4

LIFE CYCLE

Orangutans come together to **mate**. But they reproduce slowly. Females have just one baby at a time. And they only give birth about once every eight years.

A female orangutan usually has three or four babies during its lifetime.

Orangutans are born helpless. Mothers carry their babies and feed them milk for several years. They teach the babies how to find food, build nests, and avoid danger.

For the first few weeks, a baby clings to its mother while she swings through trees.

Orangutans can live between 30 and 40 years in the wild.

Orangutans go off on their own after about seven years. By about 15 years, males are fully grown. Females usually **mature** a few years earlier.

TWO TYPES OF MALES

Some male orangutans grow wide pads on their cheeks. They have big throat pouches, too. These males are twice the size of females. Other males are smaller. They look similar to females.

Orangutans' cheek pads are called flanges. Males without them are known as unflanged males.

COMPREHENSION QUESTIONS

Write your answers on a separate piece of paper.

1. Write a few sentences explaining the main ideas of Chapter 4.
2. Do you think people should hunt orangutans? Why or why not?
3. How many species of orangutans are there?
   - **A.** one
   - **B.** three
   - **C.** eight
4. How could making deeper squeaks help a small orangutan avoid predators?
   - **A.** Predators could not hear the squeaks.
   - **B.** Predators could think the orangutan is too small to attack.
   - **C.** Predators could think the orangutan is too big to attack.

5. What does **habitats** mean in this book?

*People cut down trees in their **habitats**. So, the apes have fewer places to live.*

- **A.** foods that animals eat
- **B.** places where animals make their homes
- **C.** times when animals are awake and active

6. What does **reproduce** mean in this book?

*But they **reproduce** slowly. Females have just one baby at a time.*

- **A.** to run away
- **B.** to search for food
- **C.** to have young

Answer key on page 32.

GLOSSARY

coarse
Rough or scratchy-feeling.

endangered
In danger of dying out forever.

mate
To form a pair and come together to have babies.

mature
To become fully grown or developed.

predators
Animals that hunt and eat other animals.

primates
Animals in a group that includes apes and monkeys.

species
Groups of animals or plants that are similar and can breed with one another.

tropical
Having weather that is often warm and wet.

BOOKS

Kington, Emily. *Orangutans*. Hungry Tomato, 2022.

McCarthy, Cecilia Pinto. *Rain Forest Biomes*. Abdo Publishing, 2024.

Sommer, Nathan. *Komodo Dragon vs. Orangutan*. Bellwether Media, 2021.

ONLINE RESOURCES

Visit **www.apexeditions.com** to find links and resources related to this title.

ABOUT THE AUTHOR

Trudy Becker lives in Minneapolis, Minnesota. She likes exploring new places and loves anything involving books.

INDEX

ANSWER KEY:
1. Answers will vary; 2. Answers will vary; 3. B; 4. C; 5. B; 6. C